MODAL SCALE WORKOUT

An Introduction to Modes and Scale Theory

Craig W. Smith

The Modal Scale Workout

An Introduction to Modes and Modal Scale Theory for Guitarists

Craig W. Smith

Also by Craig W. Smith:

The 7 Day Practice Routine for Guitarists (2018) 92 Pages

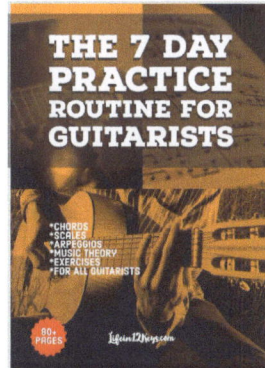

Guitar Chords for Beginners (2019) 36 Pages

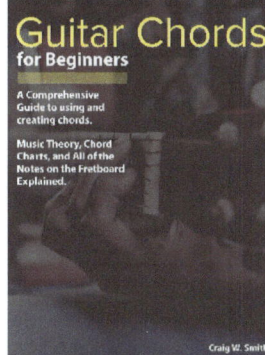

Classical Guitar - A Practical Guide Vol. 1 (2020) 129 Pages

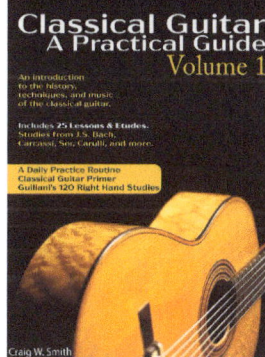

Check out the Life In 12 Keys Guitar Book Store:
http://Books.Lifein12Keys.com

Table of Contents

Preface

Back in the 1990s, I was teaching guitar lessons at Lentine's Music in Akron, Ohio. I was teaching 6 days a week and playing gigs at night on the weekends. Before the internet, before cell-phones, before YouTube... you had to take lessons in person, from an actual person.

I have a lot of great memories from those years. At one point I had over 70 students per week and a waiting list of another 20-30 people waiting for cancellation spots. As much as I'd like to think I was good at my job, the truth is; I was learning just as much from my students as they were learning from me. I still feel that way today.

This 'Modal Workout' started off as a hand written scribble on some music paper that I handed out to advanced students as a challenging exercise. The 'workout' provided the additional benefit of memorizing sequences and shapes in a key. Very useful for building improvisational skills and a strong technical foundation.

When I started my website www.LifeIn12Keys.com, one of the first things I offered to the wonderful guitarists who joined my email list was this Modal Workout. A simple 2 page PDF. No instructions, no explanation, no text; just the same exercise I was handing out to students over 25 years ago.

The funny thing was, people still loved it!

Last week I was doing some website maintenance and noticed something that struck me. The little Modal Workout I started back in the 90s had gotten over 20,000 downloads. (!!!)

I finally got around to organizing it a bit better and with more explanation and thoughts on Modal Scales in general. I took a few excerpts from my online lessons and included them here as accompaniment to fill things out.

Lastly, I added 2 additional workouts. My new Modal Workout 2.0 and an advanced version I do myself called, 'The Whole Enchilada'.

There is much to explore down the modal theory rabbit-hole. I offer only the tip of the iceberg in this little guide. As always, I encourage you to take your own studies deeper and beyond what you can get from any one source.

Most of all, enjoy the journey!

Craig Smith
July 3rd, 2020

Introduction

I know what you're thinking. 'Oh, great. Another book on scales'. You may be asking yourself the usual questions:

- Why do I need to learn these scales?
- Why do they have such funny names?
- Are these scales really going to make me better?
- Can I really use modes in everyday guitar playing situations?

These are the same things I asked myself over 30 years ago when I first started using the Modal Scales in my everyday playing.

I remember back in the late 1980's when I was first starting out on the guitar, reading about these mysterious scales in magazine interviews with guitar giants such as Randy Rhoads, Joe Satriani, Steve, Vai and Frank Zappa.

Growing up on a steady diet of Classic Rock, Blues, and Metal, it would seem everything I needed could be found inside Pentatonic, "Blues Box" shapes. Wow, was I wrong!

After playing guitar for a few years and taking my own studies deeper into music theory and improvisation, I would find more and more new shapes and ideas that would center around a Modal approach to writing and improvising.

In this guide, I hope to spark the same fire in you that I found when I first discovered modal scales.

What Can Modes Do For You?

There are many ways in which to use modal scales both as a musical device to achieve a certain mood or texture, as well as a tool from which you can cover the entire guitar fretboard in any key or scale using symmetrical patterns.

For the purposes of this book, we will be talking primarily about the latter. Using modes around a Key Center from which to build solos, melodies, riffs, and other melodic functions.

How many patterns do you need to learn? **Seven to be exact**. Yes, thats it. 7 simple patterns. But wait, theres more....

Inside these 7 Modal Scale patterns lie all of the chords, arpeggios, Pentatonic Scales and literally everything else you can do in a given key.

By learning the 7 Modal Scale patterns you are in essence creating a fool-proof blueprint from which to play all of the "good notes" all over the guitar neck... and thats just the beginning.

Once you're comfortable with different modes, you can substitute and super-impose other modes to achieve a greater sophistication in your soloing and compositions. More on that later...

Practicing Modal Scales also has a wonderful side effect which should become apparent even on your first day. Technique building, chops exploding, strengthening of both hands!... and that frankly, is the easy part. There is just no downside to getting these scales under your fingers.

About This Book

If you've read my other books, especially "The 7 Day Practice Routine For Guitarists", you know I'm a big proponent of music theory. I love to use simple music theory concepts to make guitar playing easier. Yes, I said EASIER.

A little theory goes a long way. Just in case you don't have the other book, I'm going to cover some basic harmony and scale theory (in this book) so that we can make more sense of modal scales and how they relate to chords and arpeggios in any given key.

Here are some theory concepts I will cover that are repeated from my previous book:

- The Circle of Keys
- Major Scale Harmony & Modes
- The Harmonic Minor Scale & Modes
- The Melodic Minor Scale & Modes

An edited version of the 'Thursday Scale' chapter from "The 7 Day Practice Routine" is included here for ease of use and clarification as it pertains to the modal scales.

Some Thoughts On Technique

I'm also a firm believer in technique and using good technical habits as a means to a more fulfilling musical end.

I like to think of it like a fast sports car. A Ferrari can easily hit 200+ MPH, but that really fun spot is the 80-100 MPH zone. Feel how it corners, how it responds with ease because you're not even touching what that engine can do yet.

A guitarist with solid technique functions in much the same way. No, I don't mean speed necessarily, although faster guitar playing is certainly a by-product of good technical habits. I like to think of it as more of an "ease of use" thing.

When my chops are UP and my technique is solid, everything is just easier. Everything. I'm running 80 MPH on an engine capable of much, much more. Thats what technique does for your guitar playing. All it requires is some careful repetition and time.

Alternate Picking

Throughout this book you'll see notes and instruction on alternate picking. Since this book deals primarily with scales, we will use alternate picking throughout.

If you're not familiar with alternate picking, its probably exactly what you think it is. Alternating DOWN and UP strokes with your pick. As always, using a metronome is certainly encouraged.

When alternate picking with a metronome, set it to a speed that is comfortable to play 4 notes per click (16th note feel). The down-strokes will fall on beat 1 and 3. Upstrokes on 2 and 4.

What is a Scale?

By definition, "In music theory, a scale is any set of musical notes ordered by fundamental frequency or pitch. A scale ordered by increasing pitch is an ascending scale, and a scale ordered by decreasing pitch is a descending scale"

Or in lay terms, alphabetically from A to G.

For example the C Major Scale:
C D E F G A B C

The Major scale is the foundation for all other scales, chords arpeggios.. really anything you're going to do on the Guitar (or any other instrument).

The Major Scale:

- A Major Scale has 8 notes in alphabetical order.
- Has a set interval pattern, (the space between scale tones) for every key:

Whole, Whole, Half, Whole, Whole, Whole, Half

If you're completely new to music theory, think of a whole step as 2 frets distance on the guitar and a half step as 1 fret.

There are always half steps between the notes **B-C** and **E-F**.

The Circle of Keys

The Circle of Keys (often called the Circle of 5ths), is a kind of calculator to determine the notes in any Major Scale.

The Major Scale consists of 7 different notes and one octave note in alphabetical order.

Remember that the formula for a Major Scale is:

Whole, Whole, Half, Whole, Whole, Whole, Half

Remember that a whole step, (Whole Tone) is equal to 2 frets distance, while a half-step, (Semi-Tone) equals only 1 frets distance.

With this knowledge you could build a Major Scale off of any note, providing you stick with the above formula.

When you apply this formula starting on the note C proceeding through the musical alphabet you can see how this works:

I.	C to D is a Whole Step.
II.	D to E is a Whole step
III.	E to F is a Half-Step
IV.	F to G is a Whole Step
V.	G to A is a Whole Step
VI.	A to B is a Whole Step
VII.	B to C (octave) is a Half -Step

Being able to figure out scales in this manner is a valuable tool that can be applied to any instrument. For the guitar, it is a slow process that can be averted by the use of patterns and modes.

Circle of Keys

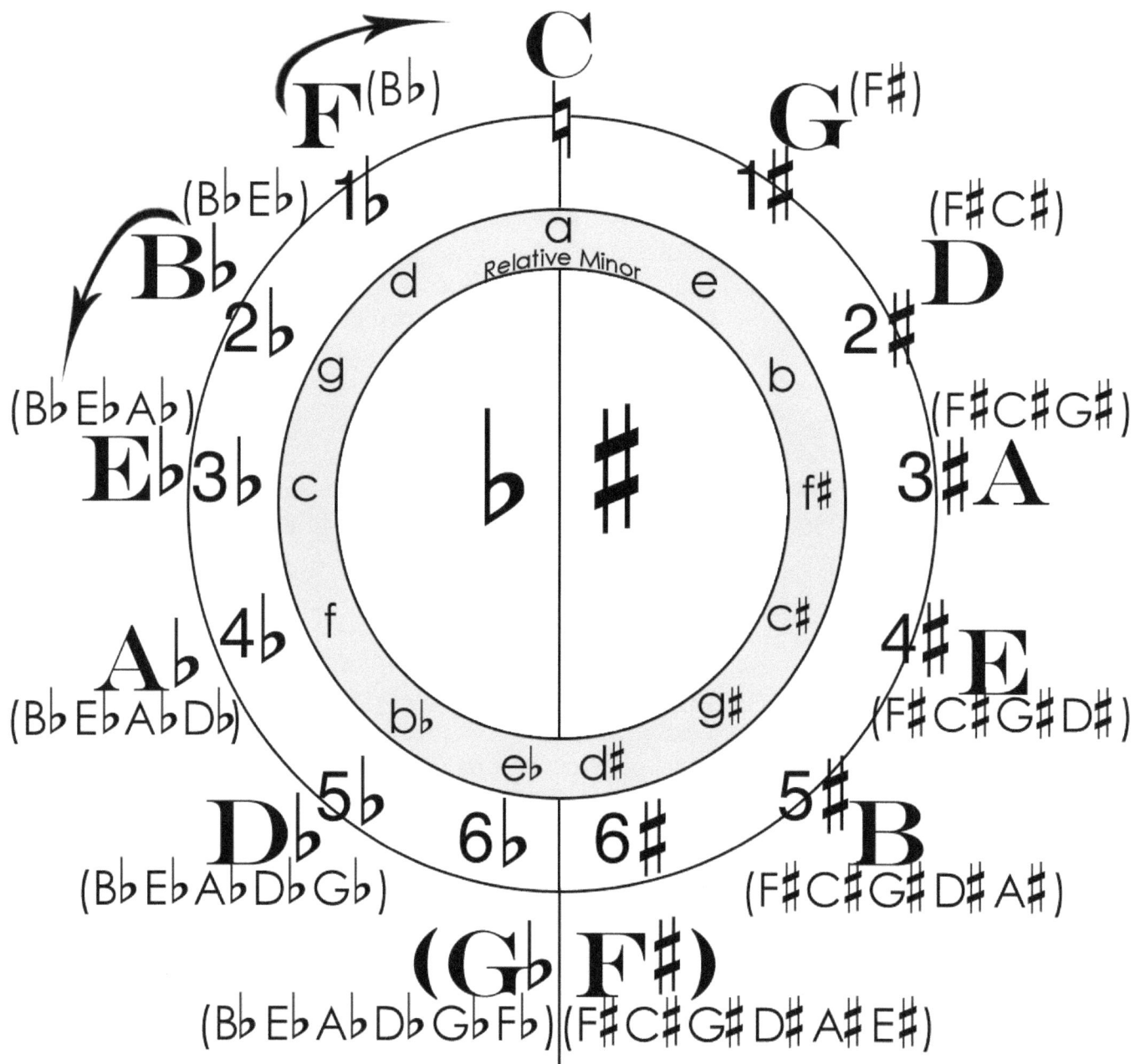

C

F (B♭)

G (F#)

(B♭ E♭) 1♭

1# (F#C#)

B♭

D

2♭

2# (F#C#G#)

(B♭E♭A♭)

E♭ 3♭

3# **A**

a

Relative Minor

d · e

g · b

c · f#

f · c#

b♭ · g#

e♭ · d#

♭ · #

A♭ 4♭

4# **E**

(B♭E♭A♭D♭)

(F#C#G#D#)

D♭ 5♭

5# **B**

6♭ · 6#

(B♭E♭A♭D♭G♭)

(F#C#G#D#A#)

(G♭ | F#)

(B♭ E♭ A♭ D♭ G♭ F♭) (F#C#G#D#A#E#)

How the Circle Works

The Sharp Side

Starting at the top of the circle with the Key of C Major, notice the natural sign indicating a key signature of NO sharps and NO Flats.

This means that if we start a scale on "C" ascending in alphabetical order, we end up with:
C D E F G A B C without having to change anything.

As we travel clockwise in 5th's to the next note "G", we add 1 sharp note.

The first sharp note is F#, indicated by the arrow pointing clockwise.
After we add the F#, we end up with a G Major Scale: **G A B C D E F# G**.

Continuing on to the next key clockwise, we get the key of D Major.

D Major contains 2 sharp notes, F# and C#.
Remember when we need to add a sharp, start on F#, then follow the arrow clockwise and add the next one in 5ths.

We end up with **D E F# G A B C# D**.

Try playing these notes on the guitar and notice how our Major Scale Formula remains intact.

Proceeding to our next Key, A Major, we add another sharp for a total of 3.
Starting on F#, following the arrow clockwise and adding C# and D#.

A Major Scale: **A B C# D E F# G# A**

Can you see the pattern forming here?

Some Important Points to Remember:

- The Major scales always contain 8 notes in alphabetical order.
- We always start on 'F' when adding sharps, adding additional ones in 5ths, or clockwise, following the arrow.
- The finished product ALWAYS falls into our Major Scale Formula: **Whole, Whole, Half, Whole, Whole, Whole, Half.**

The Flat Side

We build "flat" Keys in much the same way that we did with the sharp side of the circle, but with two important differences:

1.   Bb is the first flat note.
2.   We add our flat notes counter-clockwise (in 4ths) indicated by the arrow above Bb.

For the key of F Major, we add 1 flat note.

The first flat note is Bb.
So our F Major Scale looks like this: **F G A Bb C D E F**

Our second flat KEY "Bb", has 2 flat notes: Bb and following the arrow counter-clockwise to Eb.

Our Bb scale looks like this: **Bb C D Eb F G A Bb.**

Proceeding a 4th counter-clockwise to Eb we now need 3 flat notes to complete our scale.

Following the arrow we get Bb, Eb and Ab.

The Eb Major Scale: **Eb F G Ab Bb C D Eb.**

Continue this same pattern to create the other scales on the flat side of the circle.

Things to Remember About Flat keys:

- The Major scales always contain 8 notes in alphabetical order.
- We always start on Bb when adding flat notes, adding additional ones in 4ths, or counter-clockwise following the arrow.
- The finished product ALWAYS falls into our Major Scale Formula: **Whole, Whole, Half, Whole, Whole, Whole, Half.**

You'll find that over time the Circle of Keys will just happen for you naturally. I don't feel the need to make my students strictly memorize the circle because over time, it just clicks!

Why Use The Circle?

Before we get into modes, we must first be able to establish the notes in a Major Scale. The Major scale is the foundation for everything in music, including modal scales.

What is a Mode?

Ok, so now that we have the Circle of Keys done and can figure out what the notes are in any key, lets talk about modes!

The easiest (or simplest) way to think of a mode is to just think of each mode as a new scale built on a degree of an existing Major scale.

For example, a G Major Scale consists of these notes:
G A B C D E F# G

Ionian
The first Diatonic mode Ionian, is synonymous with a Major Scale. You could call the above scale, G Major or G Ionian.

Dorian
To build the next mode, simply start on the next note (A) and build a new scale:
A B C D E F# G A - (notice I didn't change any notes)

We now have the A Dorian Scale.

Phrygian
Starting on the next note (B) we can build B Phrygian:
B C D E F# G A B (same notes, just starting on B)

We didn't change the notes, we just built a new scale on each subsequent note. A Dorian is not an A Major scale (A B C# D E F# G# A). It is simply a G Major scale starting on the second degree (A).

Lets finish the modes in the key of G:

Lydian
Starting on the 4th note, C, we can build our C Lydian Scale:
C D E F# G A B C

Mixolydian
Next up, our 5th mode is Mixolydian starting on D:
D E F# G A B C D

Aeolian
Aeolian is the relative minor or natural minor scale. The 6th note in the key of G is E, so we'll build our Aeolian scale starting there:
E F# G A B C D E

Locrian
Locrian is the last mode. The 7th note in the key of g is F#, so we'll build the scale from there.
F# G A B C D E F#

Some Thoughts on Modes

"In the theory of Western music, a mode is a type of musical scale coupled with a set of characteristic melodic behaviors. Musical modes have been a part of western musical thought since the Middle Ages, and were inspired by the theory of ancient Greek music. The word– 'mode', derives from the Latin word modus, measure, standard, manner, way, size, limit of quantity, or method"

Funny names, hard to spell. Who cares? Well, the Ancient Greeks were on to something despite the difficult names. Why not just number them? Music theory, especially those topics pertaining to the Major Scale and modes have been basically unchanged for over 500 years. Yes, 500 years!

There are so many different ways to think of modes. Heres a random example:

- A Dorian is the 2nd Mode of the Key of G.
- You could think of A Dorian as an A Major Scale with a b3 and b7, or just think of it as the second mode (ii minor) in G Major.
- I could also think of A Dorian as an A Natural Minor Scale with a raised 6th. Mind blown!

How you visualize what a mode is in relation to what you're using it for will determine whether you think of it as relating to the key of (A) Major or minor... or just a mode of G Major.

For example, if I'm playing over a simple A minor chord vamp, I could theoretically play any A minor type scale or mode such as A minor Pentatonic, A Dorian, A Phrygian, A Aeolian, etc, al.

The flip side to that example is, I can also play any OTHER mode in G Major over that same A minor chord vamp.

Why does that work?

- A minor is the ii minor chord in G Major.
- All of the notes in an A minor chord (A C E) exist within the G Major scale.
- Therefore, the G Major scale covers all of the notes in the A minor chord (and then some). G A B C D E F# G

The Key Center Approach

The other way that just works is, all of the modes contain the same 7 notes!

For the purposes of this book I'm going to use Modal Scales using a "Key Center" approach. This essentially breaks up the guitar neck into 7 Modes per Major Key. All 7 Modes will be in the same Key and played on their respective root notes of each scale degree.

Modes in the Key of G Major:

      I.   G Ionian
      II.   A Dorian
      III.   B Phrygian
      IV.   C Lydian
      V.   D Mixolydian
      VI.   E Aeolian
      VII.   F# Locrian

When I'm using the "Key Center Approach", I tend to think of them less as individual modes (with specific sounds and characteristics), and just part of the parent Key of G Major.

This is the easiest way to digest modal playing if you're not already intimately familiar with using modal scales.

Modal Characteristics

Let's take one more chapter to address some theoretical views on modes. All modes have distinctive characteristics and personalities that make them special and different from one another.

Lets explore some modal shapes using the key of C for all examples below:
C D E F G A B C (Parent Major Key)

In their most basic form, we can create small, single-octave modal scale shapes starting on each note of the C Major scale.

Not very practical for getting around the neck. More on that later...

Mode Formulas and Characteristics

Ionian

- Ionian is synonymous with the Major Scale. They are one and the same.
- Can use Major Pentatonic on same root.
- Ionian is a happy and bright scale. Pop, Rock, Country Music, etc.

C Major/Ionian Scale: C D E F G A B C

Dorian

- Dorian is a minor type scale.
- It is the 2nd mode in every key.
- Can use minor pentatonic on same root.
- Dorian contains a lowered 3rd and 7th degree from its Major parent scale.
- Dorian is somewhat dark and bluesy. Latin, Blues & Rock.

C Dorian - C D Eb F G A Bb

Phrygian

- Phrygian is a minor type scale.
- It is the 3rd mode in every key.
- Can use minor pentatonic on same root.
- Phrygian contains a lowered 2nd, 3rd, 6th, and 7th from its parent major.
- Very dark, almost Spanish sounding, exotic. Flamenco, Metal, Prog.

C Phrygian - C Dd Eb F G Ab Bb C

Lydian

- Lydian is a Major type scale
- It is the 4th mode in every key.
- Can use the Major Pentatonic on the same root.
- Lydian's only change from its parent Major (Ionian) is the raised 4th.
- Airy, dreamy quality.

C Lydian - C D E F# G A B C

Mixolydian

- Mixolydian is a Major type scale.
- It is the 5th mode of every key.
- Can use the Major pentatonic on same root.
- Mixolydian contains a lowered 7th from its parent major.
- Jazzy, Bluesy, more depth than Ionian.

C Mixolydian - C D E F G A Bb C

Aeolian

- Aeolian is a minor type scale. It is the relative or natural minor of every key.
- It is the 6th mode of every key.
- Can use the minor pentatonic and Blues Scale on same root.
- Aeolian contains a lowered 3rd, 6th, and 7th from its parent major.
- Darker than dorian, not as dark as Phrygian. Works well in Blues, Rock & Metal.

C Aeolian - C D Eb F G Ab Bb C

Locrian

- Locrian is a minor type scale. Can also be thought of as diminished.
- It is the 7th mode of every key.
- Pentatonic Major and minor scales do NOT work on the 7th root.
- Locrian has a lowered 2nd, 3rd, 5th, 6th, and 7th.
- Very dark!

C Locrian - C Db Eb F Gb Ab Bb C

Modes on the Guitar Neck

Sometime last year, I wrote a very popular lesson on the Lifein12keys.com Guitar Lesson Blog about different ways to look at modes on the guitar neck.

Whenever I see guitar modes explained in lessons and by other guitarists, there always seems to be one key point missing. How they overlap each other. When discussing how to use guitar modes, it's really important to understand how they fall across the fretboard in any given key.

To further illustrate this point, I received an email from an email subscriber who had just purchased my book The 7 Day Practice Routine For Guitarists. He said his guitar teacher had shown him modal scales in the old style block forms and wondered why I taught them as 3-note-per-string-shapes.

Old-School Block-Style Guitar Mode Shapes

Before we get into the bigger shapes, it's worth mentioning that these block shapes are perfectly fine and useful guitar mode shapes. In fact, I believe there is some benefit to learning both. Let's look at the old-school block style modal shapes in order in the key of G Major (G A B C D E F# G).

The squared notes indicate the root of each scale:

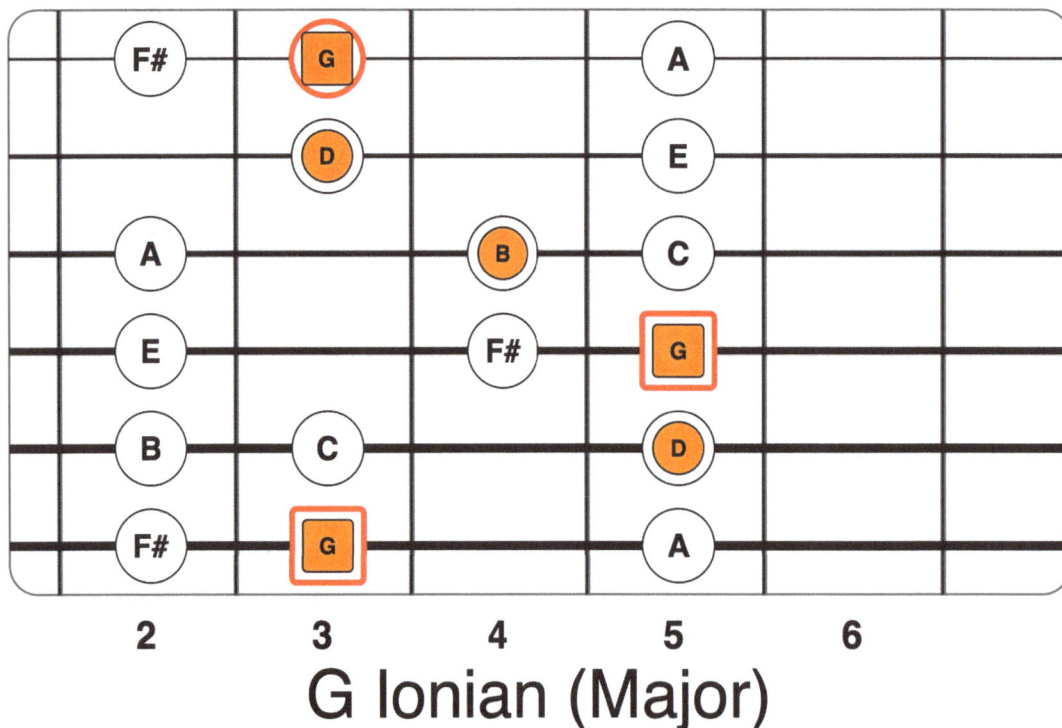

G Ionian (Major)

The thing I like about these shapes is that you can clearly see the chord form for each root note within the block shape. (colored notes)

These charts are handy because you to get chords and modes under you fingers right away.

G Major Chord form highlighted in ORANGE

Remember that Ionian is just another name for a plain old Major Scale.

A Dorian / A minor Chord

The 2nd degree A, includes a minor chord form.
Dorian is a popular minor mode often used by Carlos Santana among others.

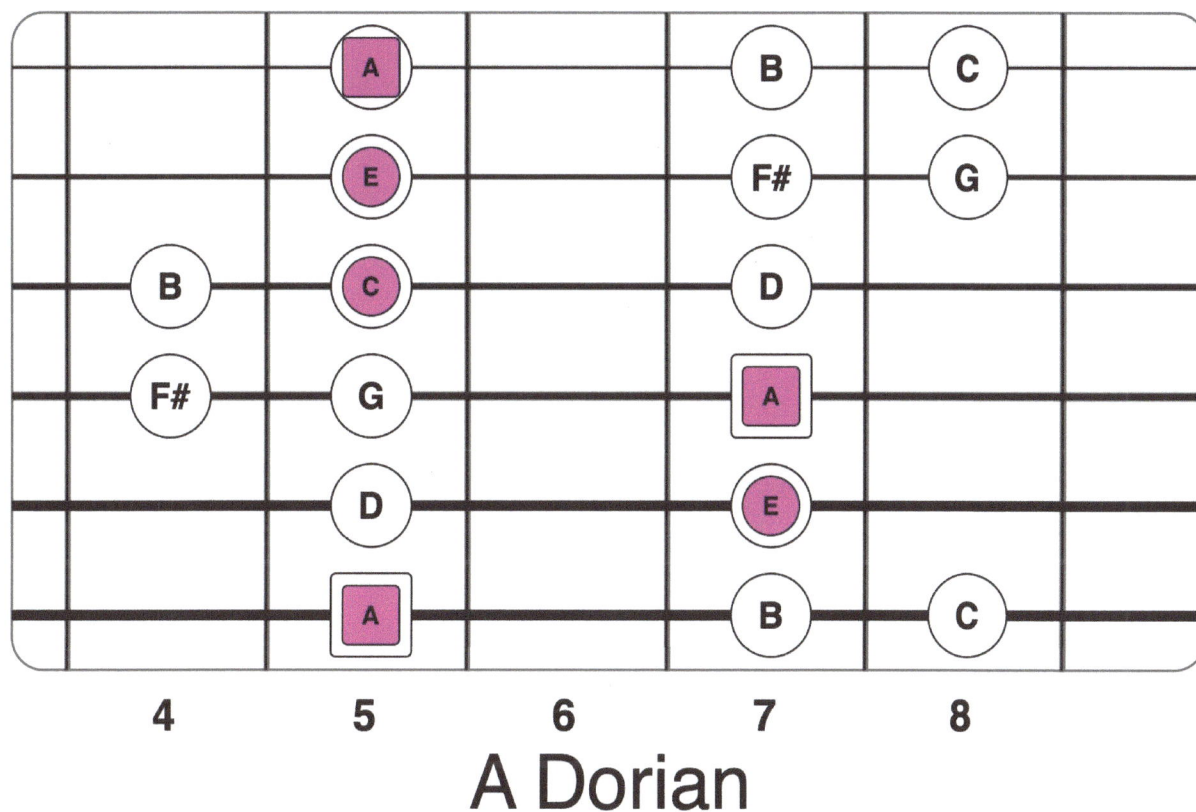

A Dorian

The 3rd degree, also a minor chord on the B root.
Phrygian is a cool sounding mode when you're trying to get a dark, almost Spanish sound.

B Phyrgian / B minor Chord

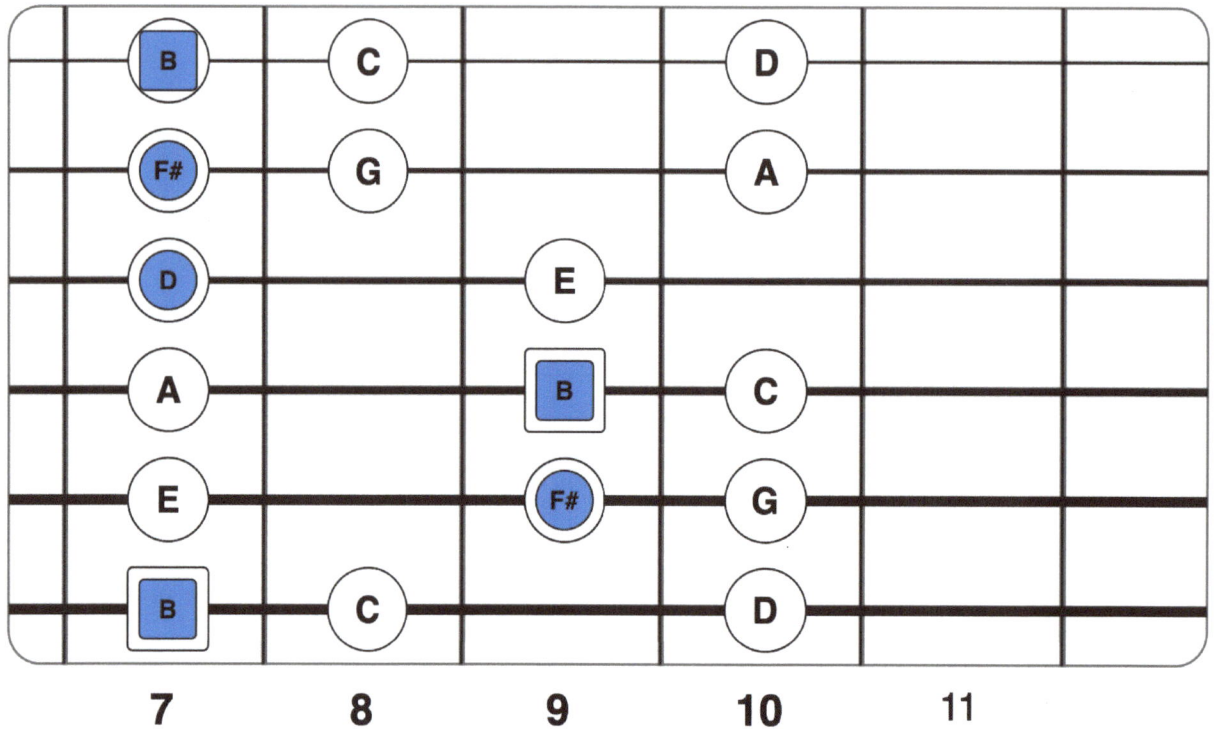

B Phrygian

C Lydian with a C Major chord.

Lydian is a great mode that exploits the b5 (#11) sound and is widely used by guitarists such as Steve Vai and Joe Satriani.

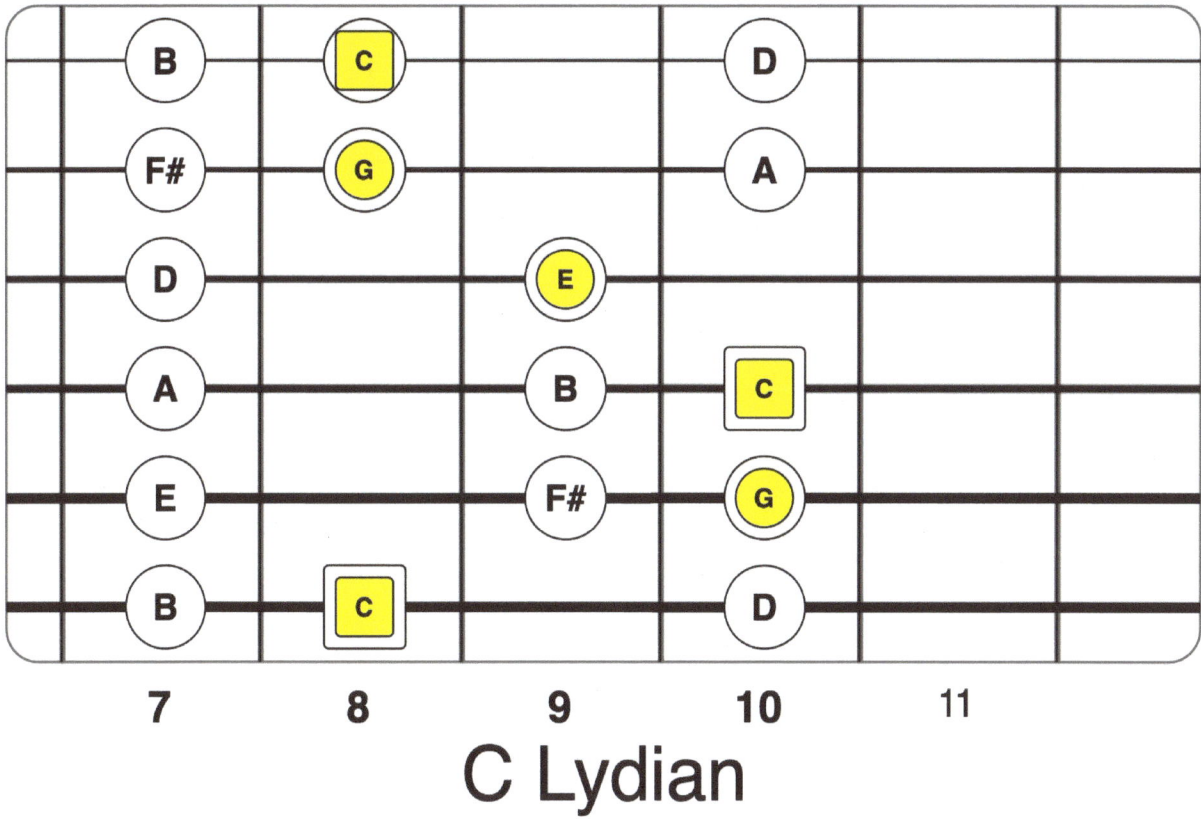

C Lydian

D Mixolydian with a D Major chord.

Mixolydian works great over dominant 7th and 9ths. Try this scale over a D7 or D9 chord or backing track.

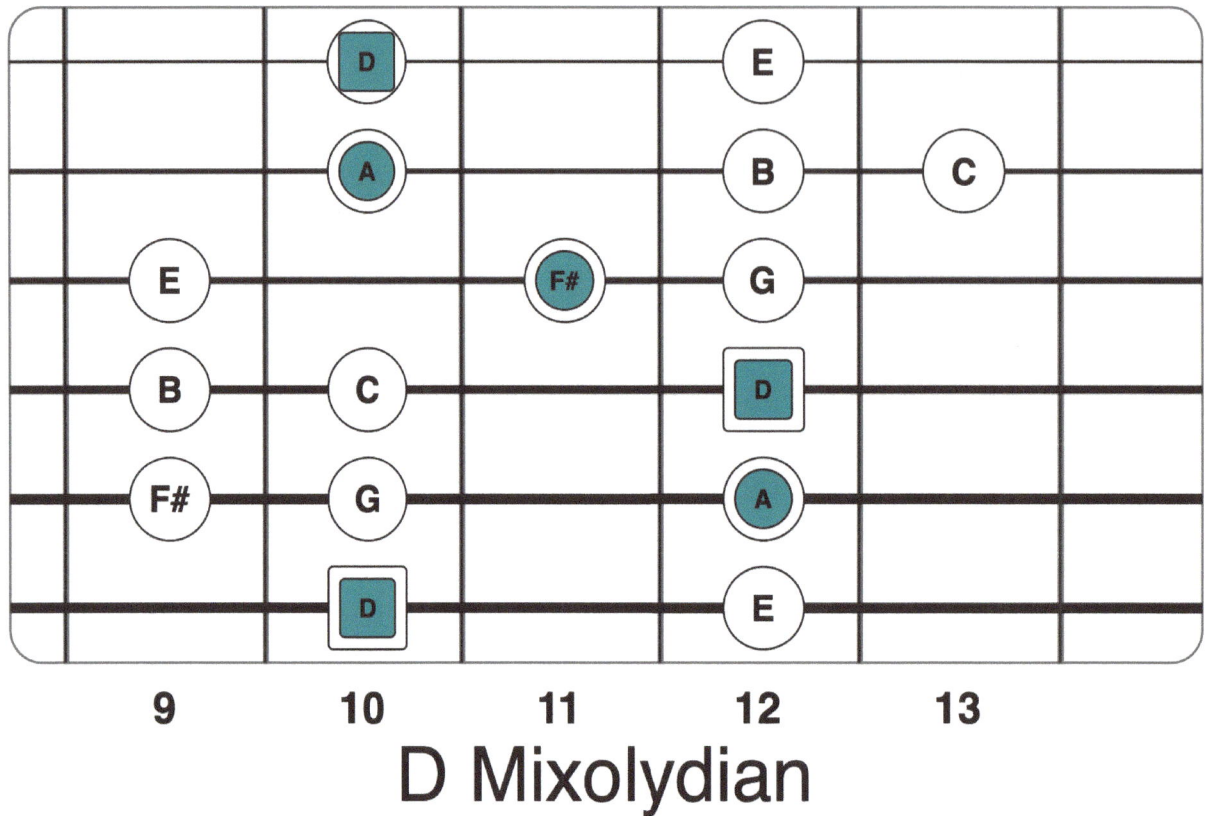

D Mixolydian

E Aeolian, a.k.a., the E Natural Minor scale and chord.

The natural minor scale works great over any minor type chord and any time you want to take some of the "happy" out of your solos. Also great for Blues.

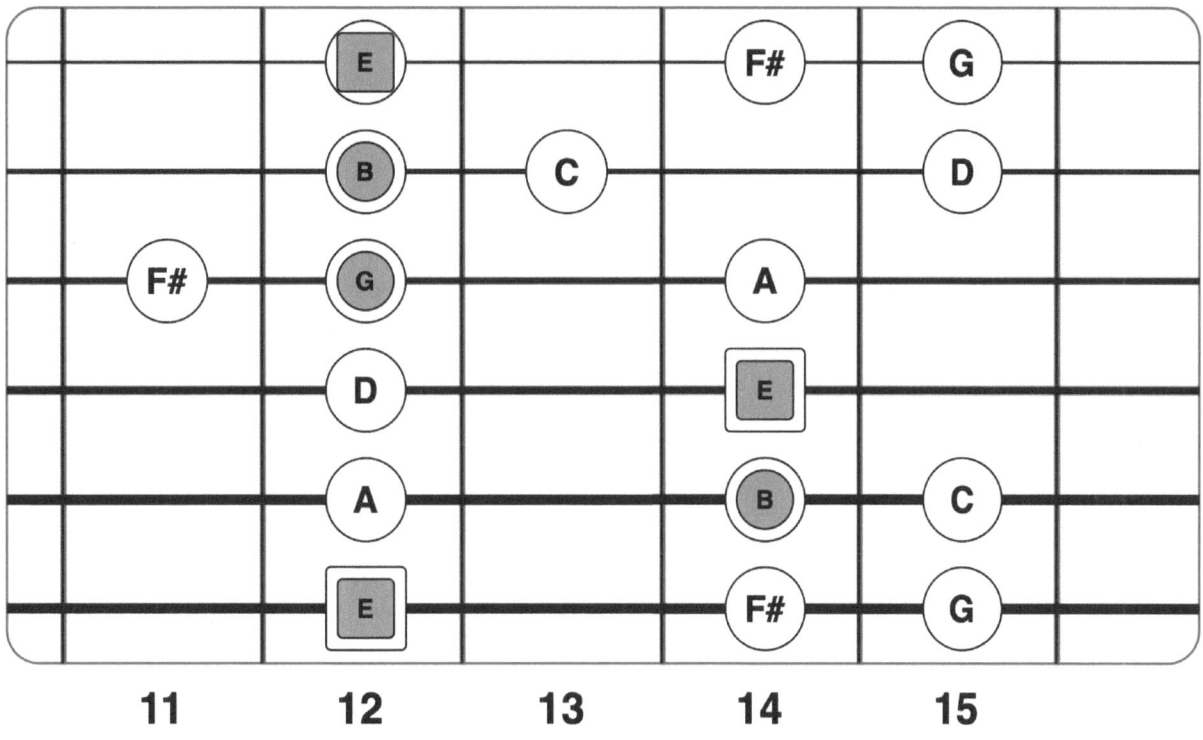

E Aeolian (Natural Minor)

F# Locrian and the diminished chord.

Having a flatted 3rd, 5th, and 7th makes for a very exotic and dark sounding scale. Use over diminished or minor 7b5 chords.

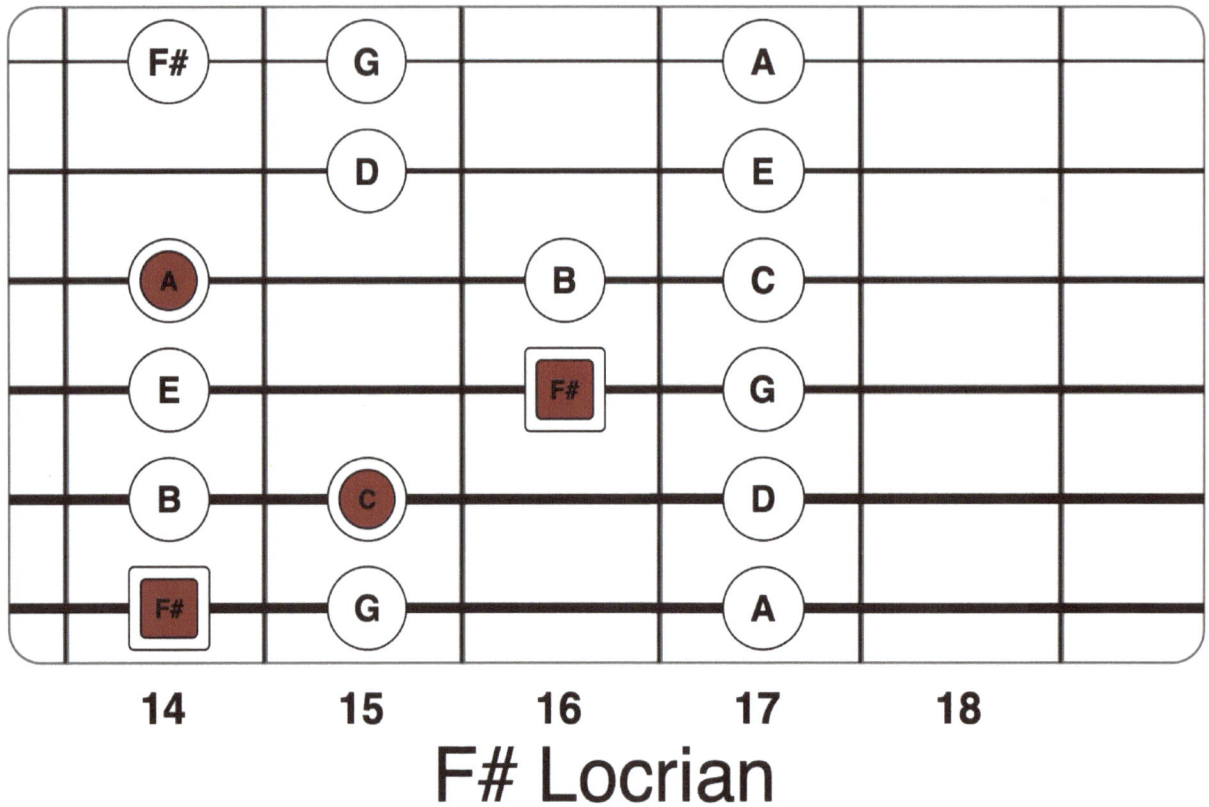

F# Locrian

Block Shapes vs. 3 Note-Per-String Shapes

Let's take a look at the difference between conventional block shapes and more modern shapes using the G Major or G Ionian Mode:

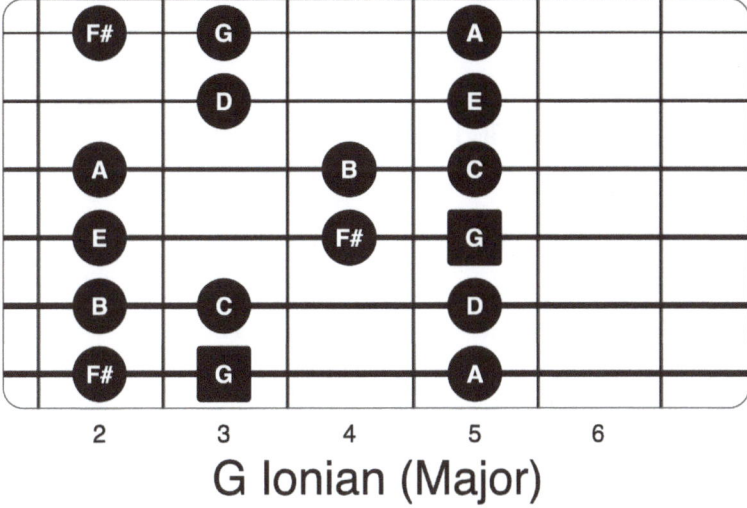

G Ionian (Major)

In this common block form, we get all of the notes in the G Major scale twice up to the high A on the 5th fret, E string.

Now let's take a look at the same G Ionian scale mapped out for **3 notes on each string**:

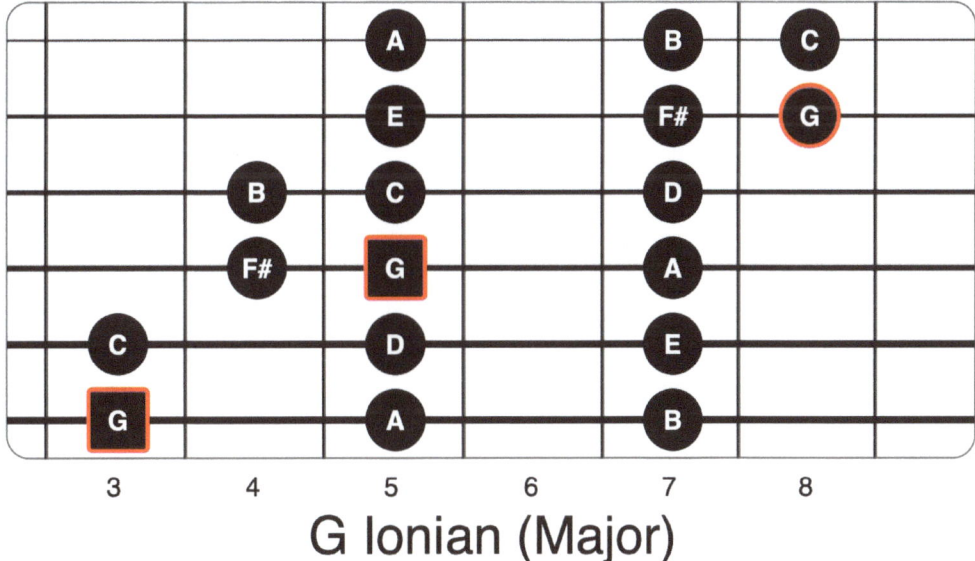

G Ionian (Major)

Lots more fretboard coverage right? You bet! Not only that, but you get a much easier to memorize symmetrical shape that includes a few extra high notes on the high E string. Don't be afraid of those 5 fret stretches. They will feel comfortable in no time with a little practice.

It came from the 80's....

...well, maybe not, but it certainly became a thing in the 1980's post Van Halen era guitar boom. What a boom it was too! Sure, guys like Al Di Meola, John McLaughlin, and other Jazz and Classical guitarists had been using shapes like these for years. It just didn't really catch on in the mainstream... and certainly not Rock guitar, until the early 1980's.

Edward Van Halen along with Randy Rhoads and later Yngwie Malmsteen, ushered forth a new revolution in Rock and Metal guitar pedagogy. Suddenly everyone was getting really, really good. They also were all using some form of a 3-note-per string scale to achieve a higher level of speed and technique than heard previously.

That's not to say, it's all about speed. Certainly not. Good technique and fretboard knowledge can be a means to an end regardless of whether you want to play "fast" or not. While 3-note-per-string scale shapes certainly make it easier to play faster, they also just cover more of the fretboard and overlap in a way that's visually easier to digest.

Let's take a look at why that is....

The Guitar Mode Overlap

Take a look at this 3-note-per-string G Ionian shape with the adjacent A Dorian mode overlapped. By 'overlapped', I mean; the natural position of both G Ionian and A Dorian in the Key of G, physically overlap eachother.

G Ionian (green) with A Dorian (black).

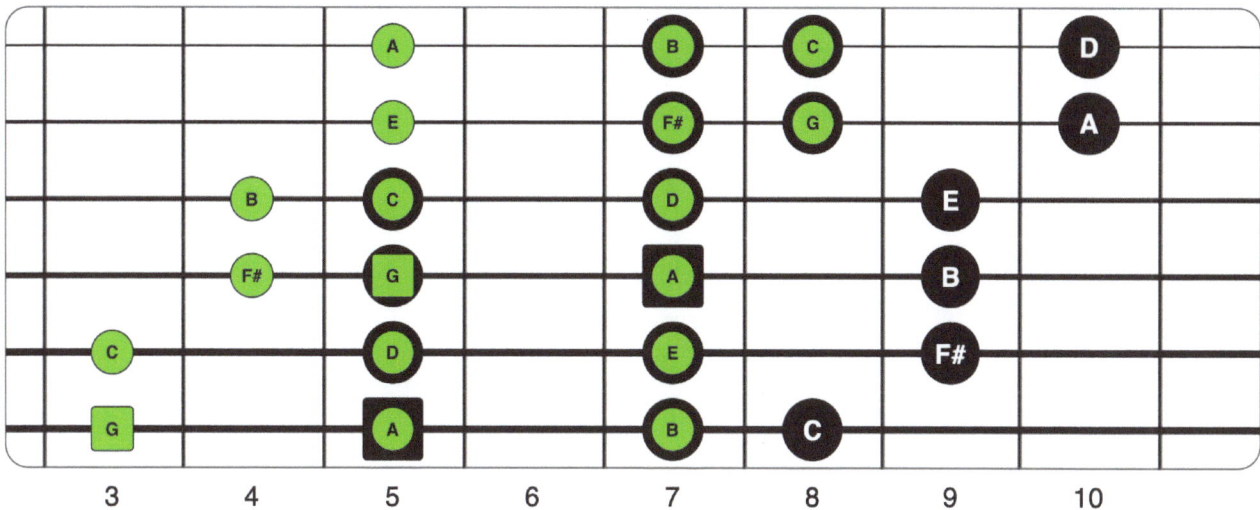

There are a few interesting and useful patterns to remember (with these shapes) to help you get the whole neck memorized in a key.

- There are always 3 notes on each string.
- The next mode always starts on the second note of whatever mode you started with. In this case the "A" note.
- You'll always get the first 2 notes of an adjacent mode from the LAST 2 notes of the mode before it.
- The first 6 notes on the low strings show up again as the same shape in the next mode's middle string set.
- The 6 notes on the middle strings show up in the NEXT mode's 2 highest string set.

A Dorian (yellow) and B Phrygian (Black) overlap in the same way!

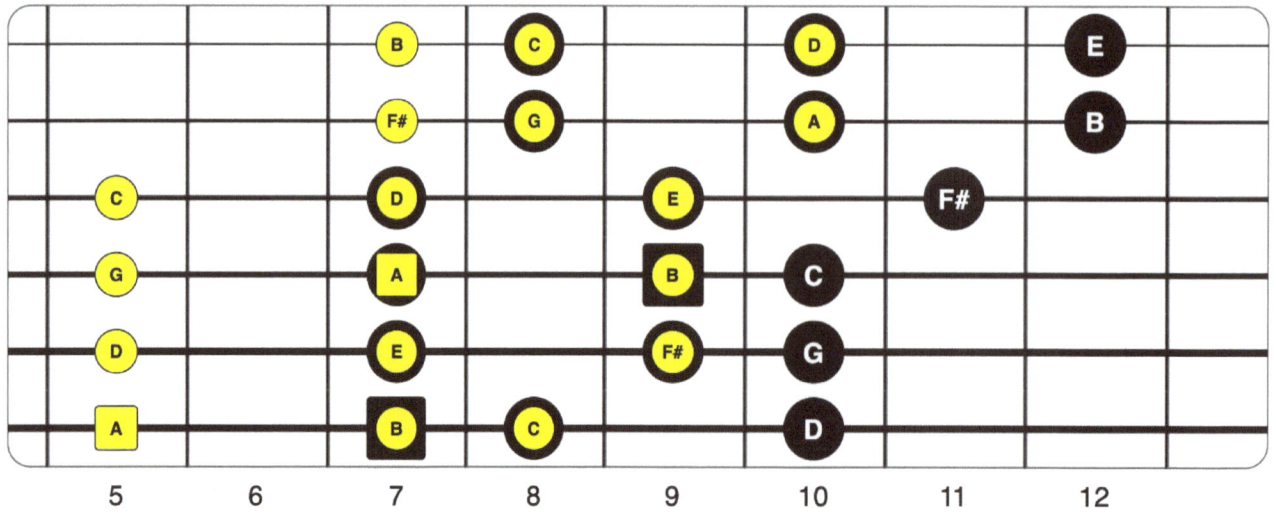

B Phrygian (Blue) and C Lydian (Black).

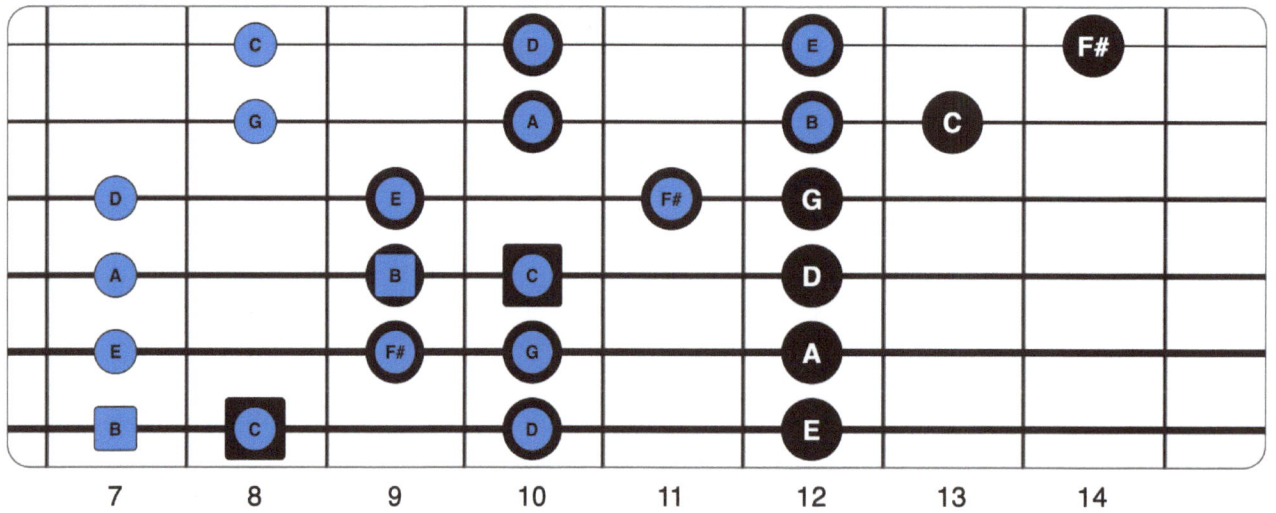

C Lydian (Orange) overlapped with D Mixolydian (Black).

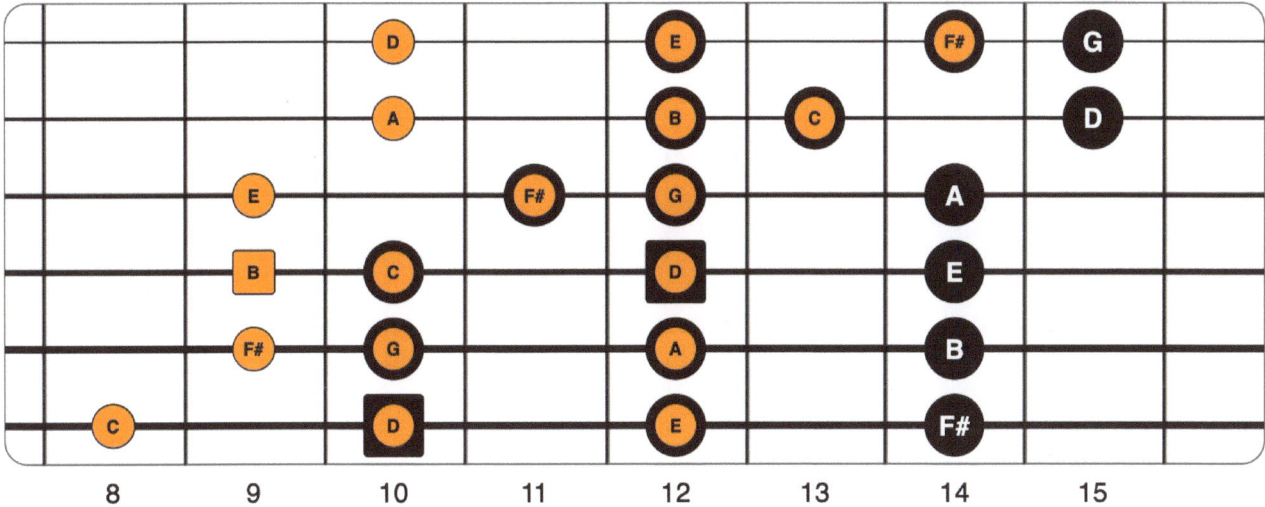

D Mixolydian (pink) overlapped by E Aeolian (black).

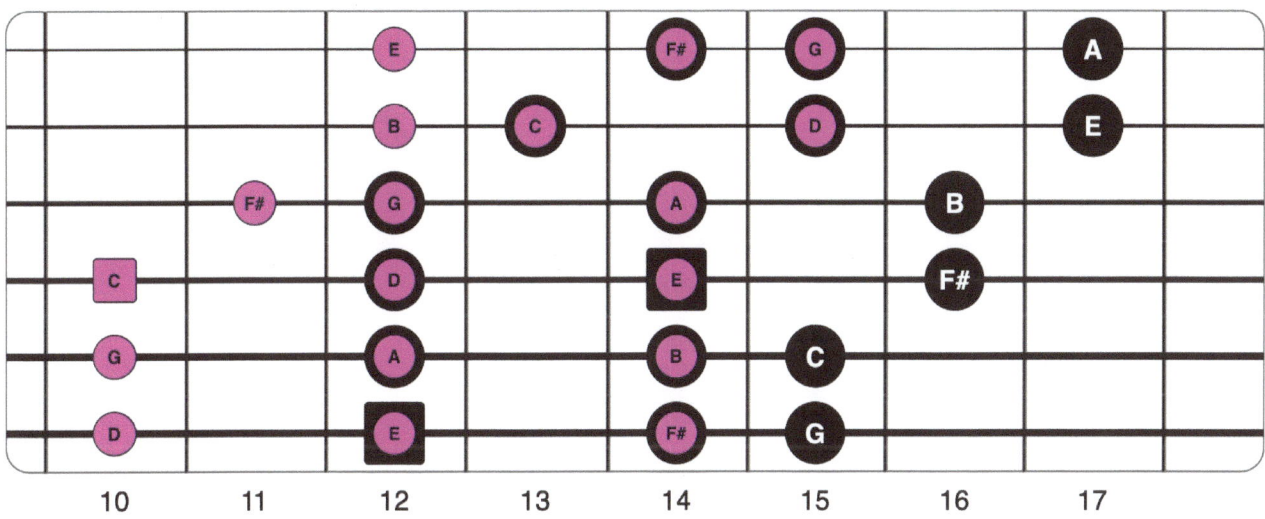

E Aeolian (Black) overlapped by F# Locrian (red).

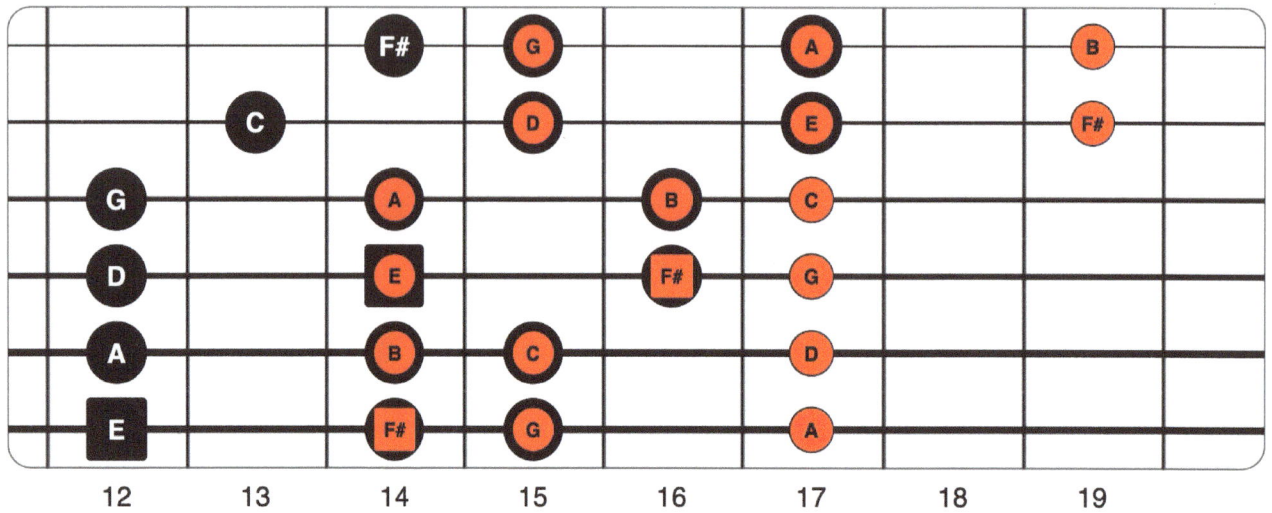

F# Locrian (black) overlapping the G Ionian mode (green). We're done! You've covered the entire neck in modal scales in the key of G Major (E minor).

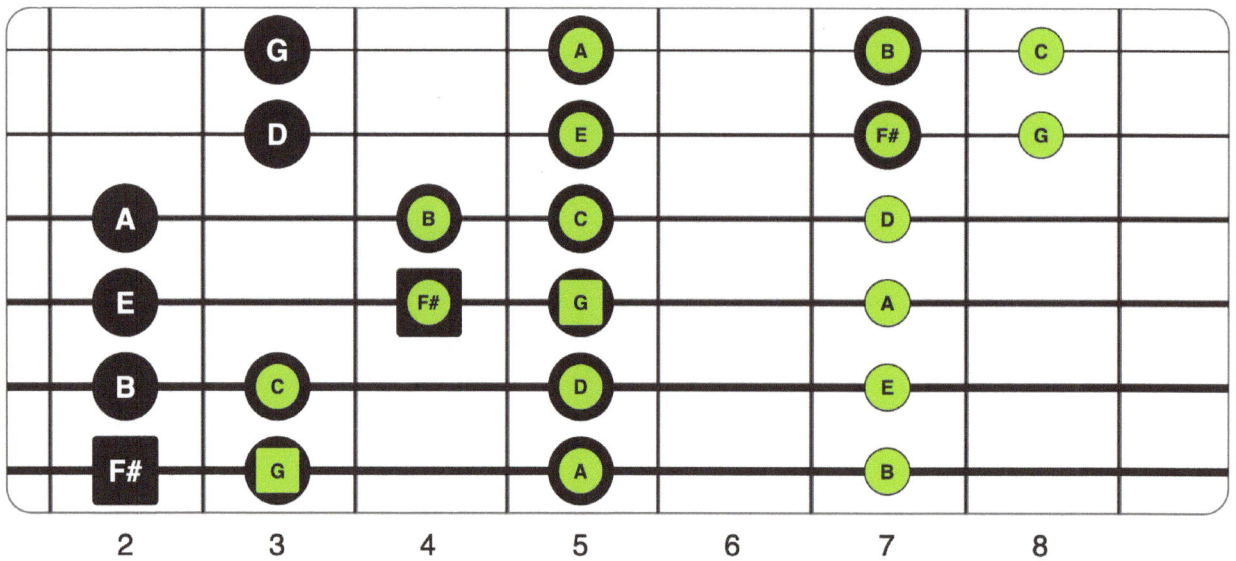

Of course this works in every key and the overlapping works and looks the same regardless of what key you're playing in.

Some Practice Tips

- Practice the "up one, down the next" exercise below to create familiarity with the shapes and overlap connections.
- Pick 2-3 chords from the block shapes above and create your own song or backing rhythm.
- If you can, record yourself. If not, grab an E minor backing track and use it for practice.
- Go through each pair of overlapping mode patterns and come up with a solo. Improvise!
- When you feel comfortable with one pair, move on to the next.

In the above exercise, we're simply travelling up one scale and down the next. Once you're comfortable with that, you're almost ready for the Modal Workout!

- Starting in Ionian, play it ascending.
- After the last note, shift to the last note in the Dorian mode and continue descending.
- After the first note in Dorian, shift to the first note in Phrygian and do it again.
- Continue the patterns through all 7 modal scales.

Modal Shapes

Putting the modal shapes onto the guitar neck is fairly painless. You could use any of the shapes we've covered thus far and you'd do just fine.

Over the years, I've seen vertical shapes, horizontal shapes, and charts that map out the modes all over the neck. In my experience teaching guitar lessons for nearly 30 years, my students have had great success with good old-fashioned vertical style shapes.

The following charts include diatonic modes for standard Major keys as well as Harmonic and Melodic minor scale modes.

I've found what works best for me (and my students) is to take 1 or 2 modes and practice between them before moving on. I like to SEE the overlap. It helps me visualize the key on the neck. After some time, you will find soloing in any key to be more comfortable, confident, and eventually effortless.

If you're completely new to modes, stick with the keys of C and G Major. You'll find these keys to be the most common on the guitar, especially in the styles of Rock, Blues, and Metal.

Once you've memorized all 7 shapes, try them in a different key. I like to alternate different keys each time I do the Modal Workout.

Sequences

One of my favorite ways to get around the neck is to create sequences using patterns found naturally inside modal scale shapes. There is no limit to what you can do with this idea, but a great place to start is with simple octave shapes.

The basic premise is to play only the first 2 strings of any mode, moving to the next set of strings in the mode that follows. In this example in the Key of G, we'll start with the lowest available mode; F# Locrian.

After playing the first 6 notes in Locrian on the low E and A strings, we'll move to the next set using the middle pattern in G ionian.
Following this pattern, we then move to the top set of strings, playing the last 6 notes of the A Dorian mode. The beauty of these sequences is, the shapes stay the same in each pair of string sets.

This is a great way to learn the neck in whatever key you want to write, solo, or improvise in. A nice side-effect is that you're building technique and getting out of single-pattern boxes. You're playing and improvising will become stronger and you'll 'SEE' the entire fretboard connected in a more intuitive way.

Spend some time with this one before moving to the actual Modal Workout.

Connecting Sequences

Key of G

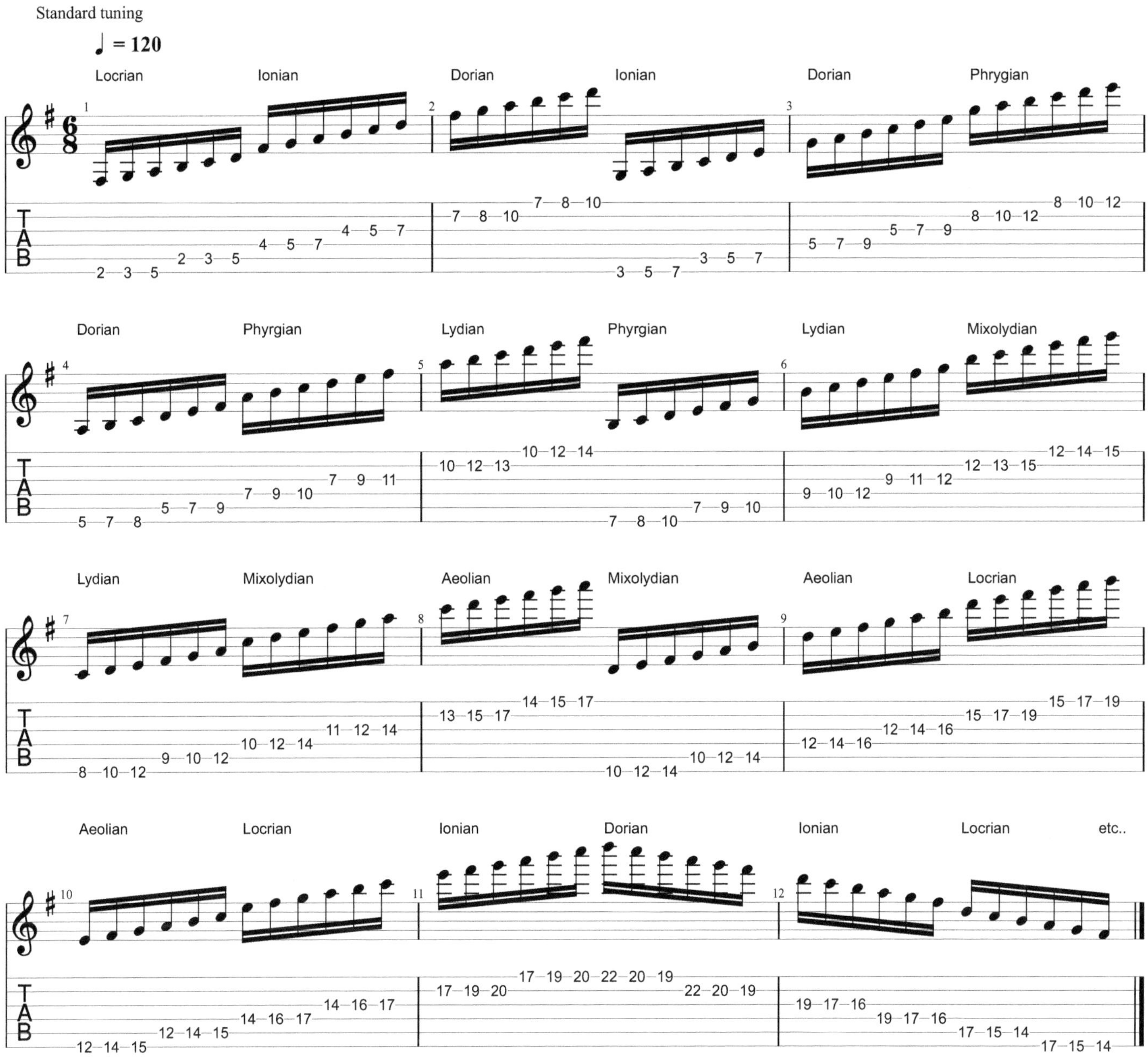

Minor Modes

Melodic Minor
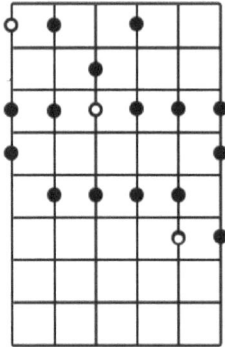

Dorian ♭2
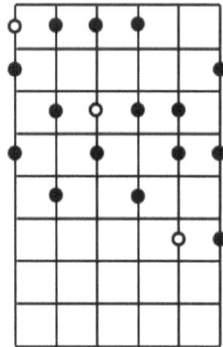

Lydian ♯5
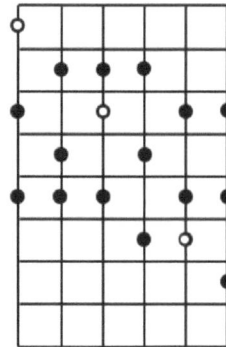

Lydian Dominant
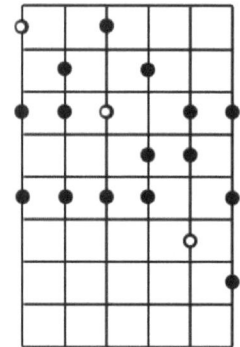

Mixolydian ♭6
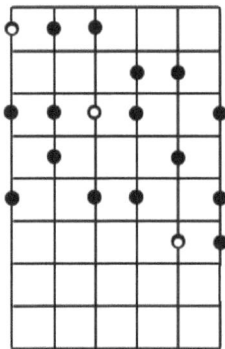

Aeolian ♭5
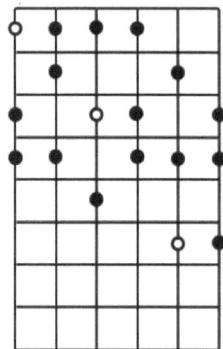

Super Locrian
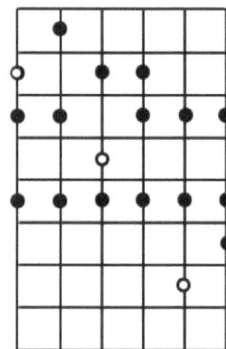

Harmonic Minor
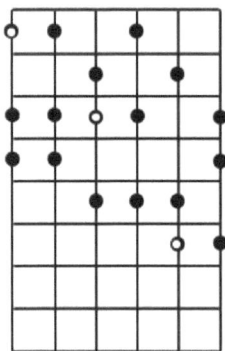

Locrian ♯6
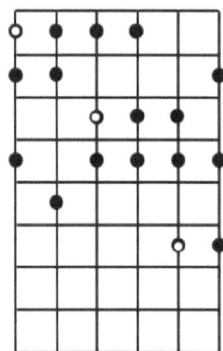

Ionian ♯5
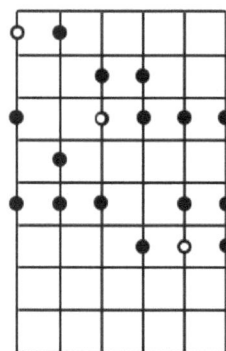

Dorian ♯4
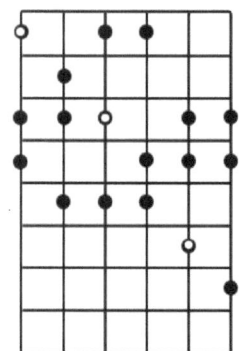

Phrygian Dominant
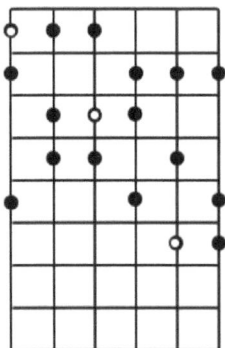

Lydian ♯2
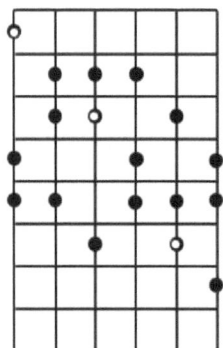

Diminished
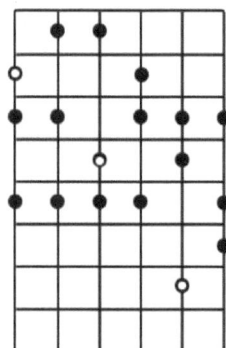

The Modal Workout

I've been doing this exercise or some variation of it, for over 25 years. It is fantastic for your left hand. It is possibly the greatest picking exercise you could ever hope to find. Best of all, you're learning while reaping tremendous technical benefits.

The following 'workout' uses the G Ionian mode. Once you're comfrotable with the entire pattern, move on to the other modes and apply it to each of them.

Sure, I could have written it out in all 7 modes, but then you would not be learning anything! You'll benefit so much more by learning it in Ionian and then applying the pattern to the other modes.

The Modal Workout 2.0

What follows the first workout is my updated 2020 version (2.0). I keep tweaking this exercise for myself to address any problems in my own picking that may pop up from time to time. You should do the same! Enjoy.

This little piece of music has had over 20,000 downloads from my website. I'm not famous and I am not some big company that churns out web content, so... I think it finally deserved a book of it's own!

The Whole Enchilada

Believe it or not, I've had guitarists email me about a more challenging exercise. 'The whole Enchilada' is the Modal Workout kicked up a notch for advanced players. I've included a longer legato section, triplets, and some challenging pedal-points at the end.

This last workout is identical to the one I do almost daily. I try to do it in all 7 modes, at least 4-5 times a week. It's all I need to keep my technique in excellent shape and tackle whatever gigs or playing challenges I have ahead of me.

As always, if you need help or have any questions, feel free to contact me anytime. I truly love to talk about guitar and help people like you. I mean it!

Email: CraigWSmith@me.com

The Modal Workout

G Ionian

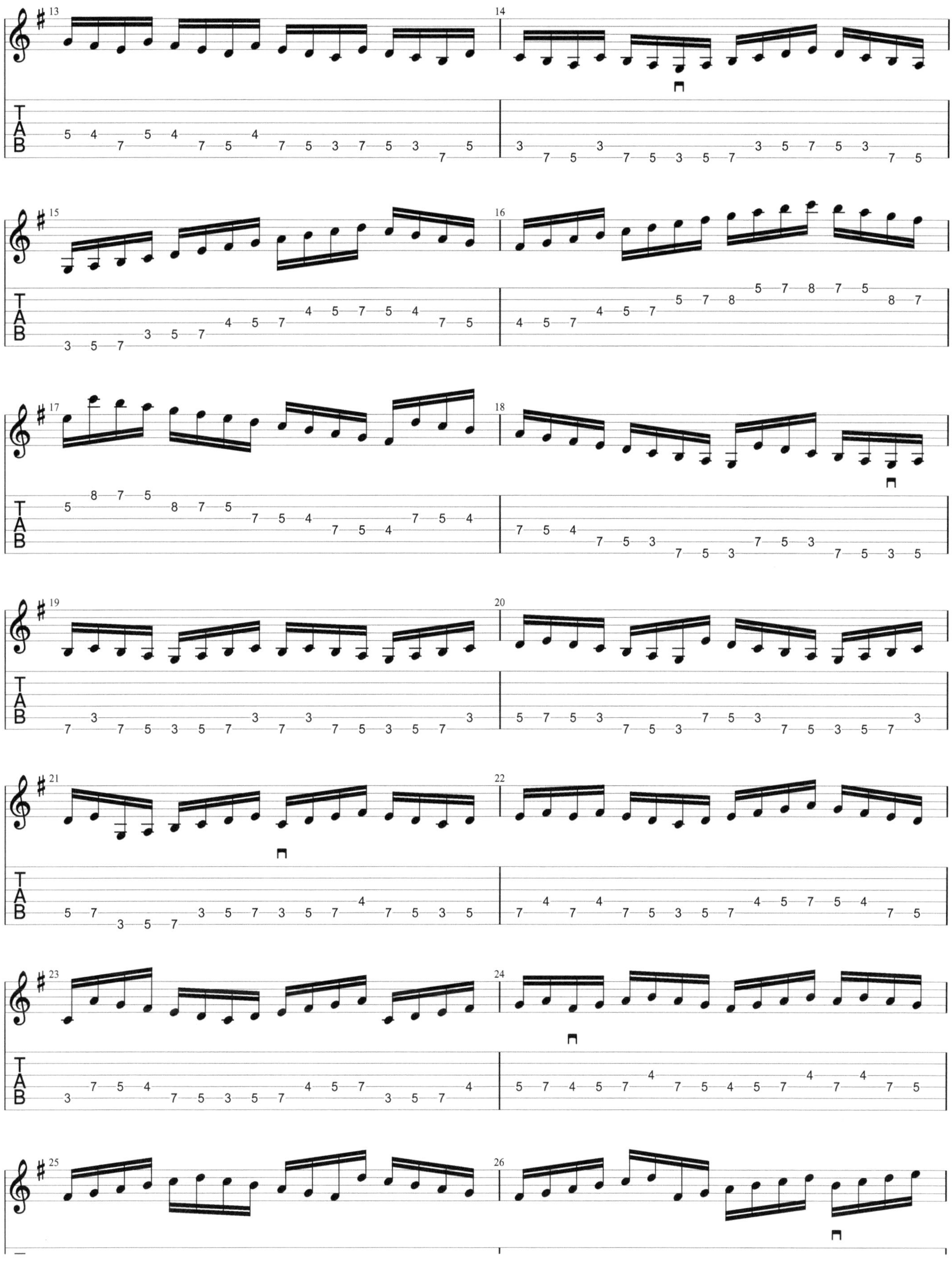

The Modal Workout 2.0
Key of G Major

41

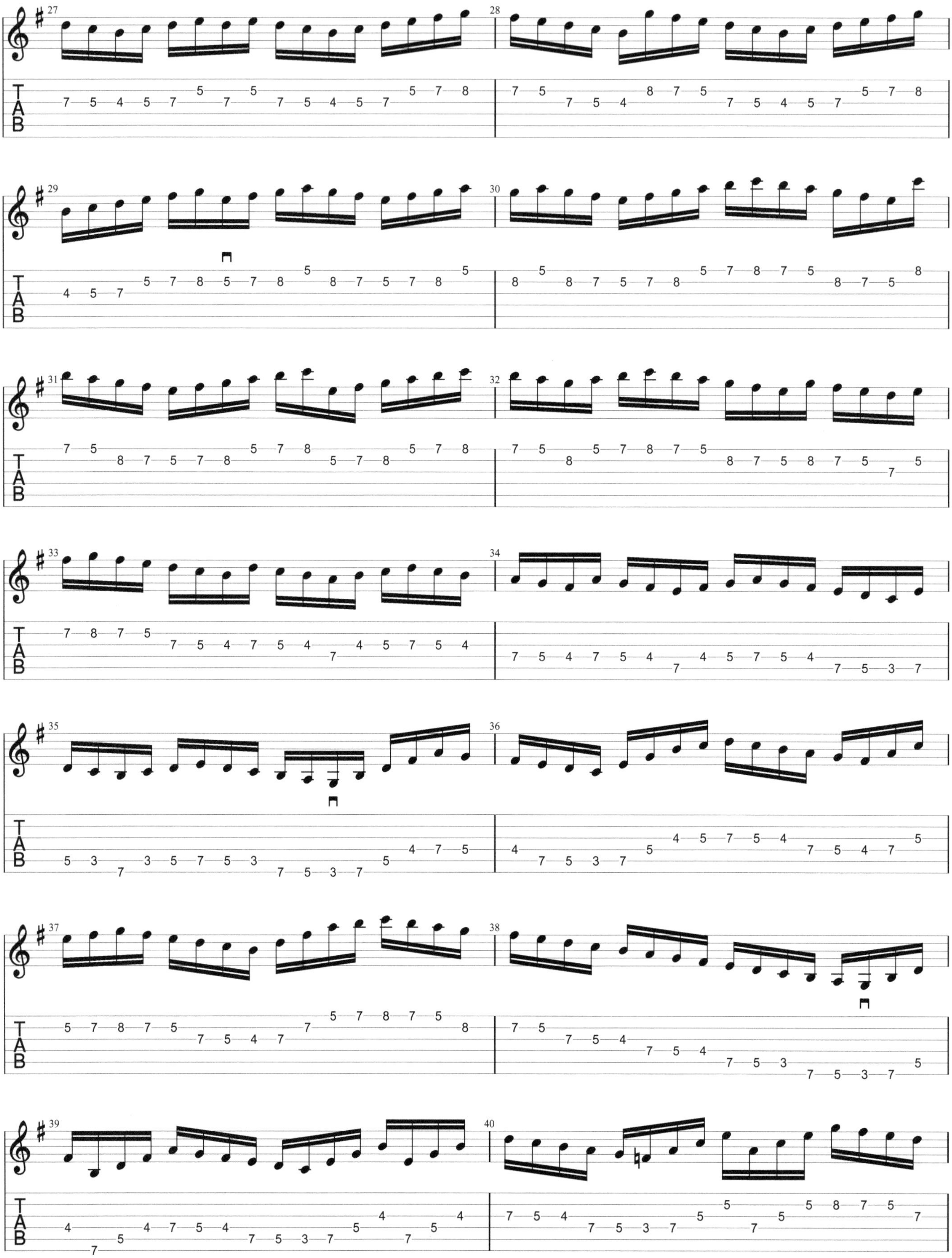

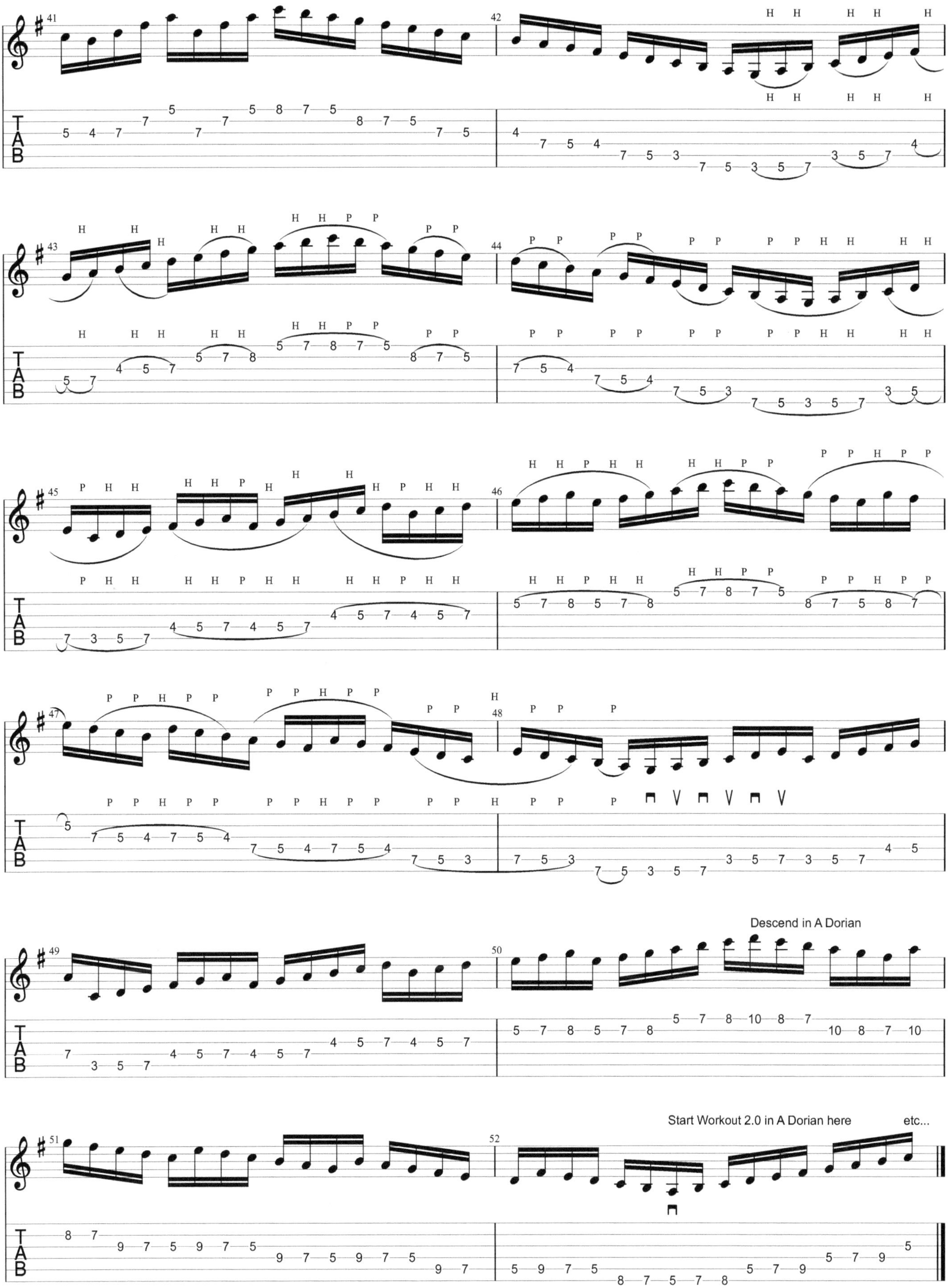
Descend in A Dorian
Start Workout 2.0 in A Dorian here
etc...

The Whole Enchilada

Key of G Major

Up & Back - Outside Picking

45

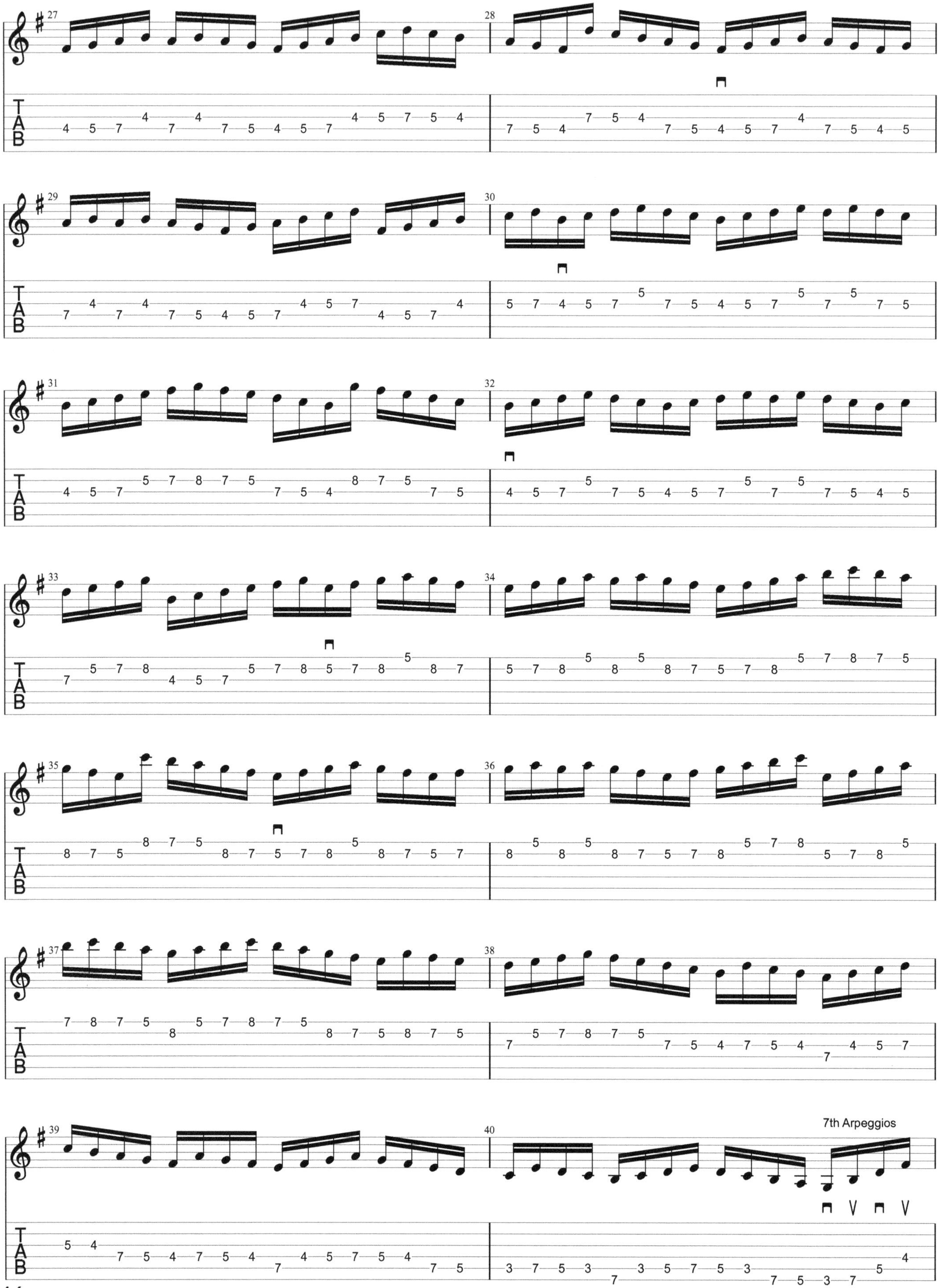
7th Arpeggios

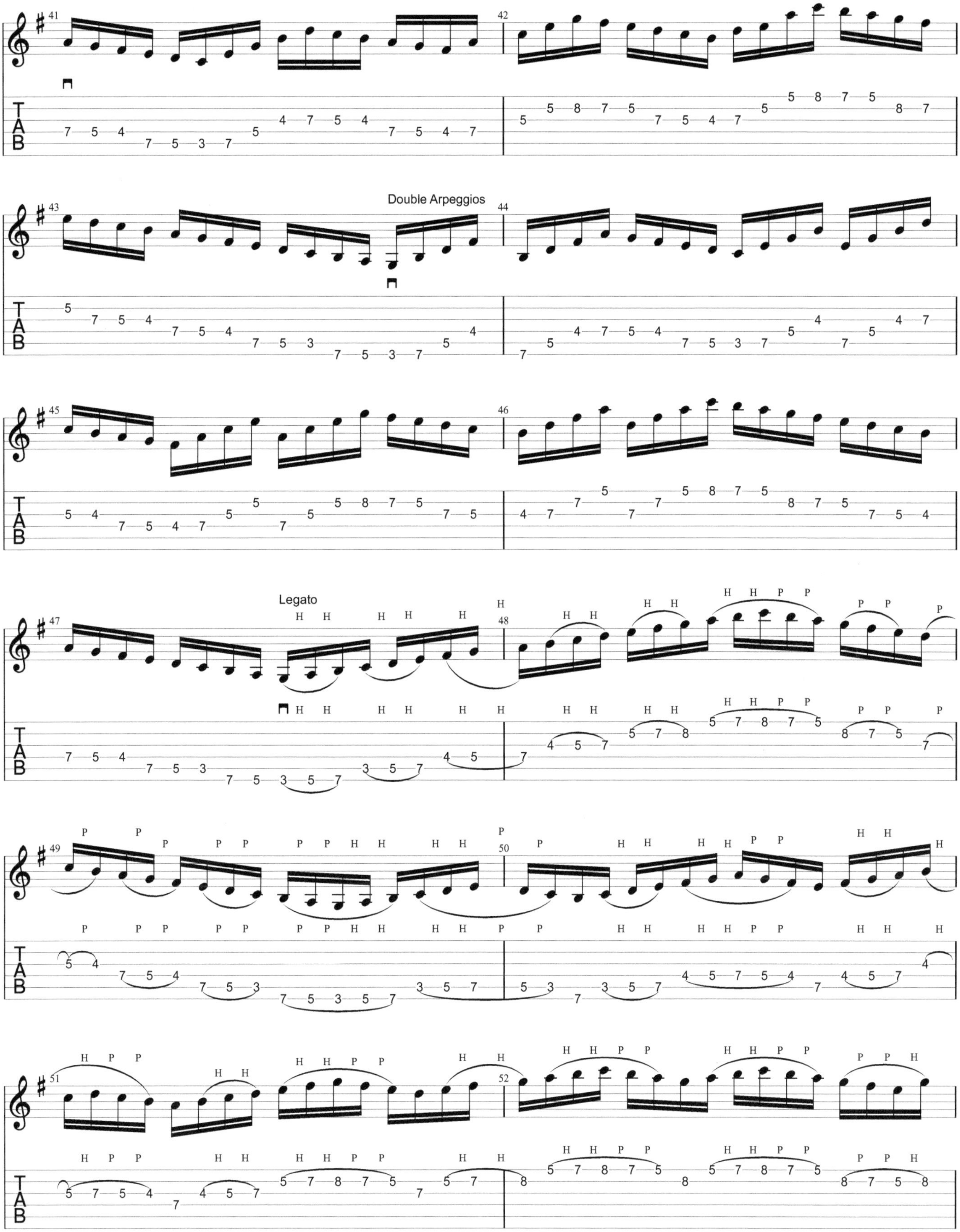
Double Arpeggios
Legato

48

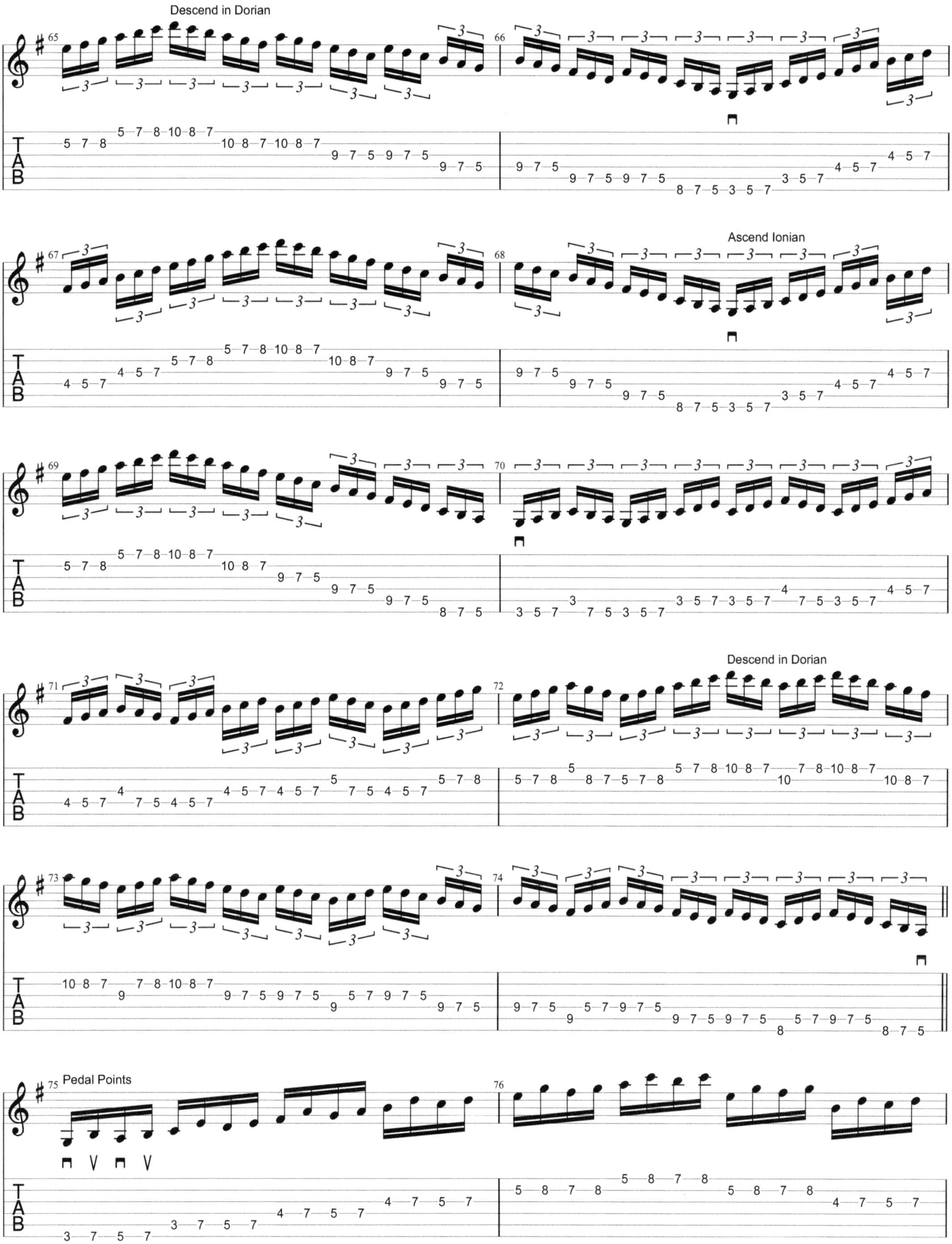
Descend in Dorian
Ascend Ionian
Descend in Dorian
Pedal Points

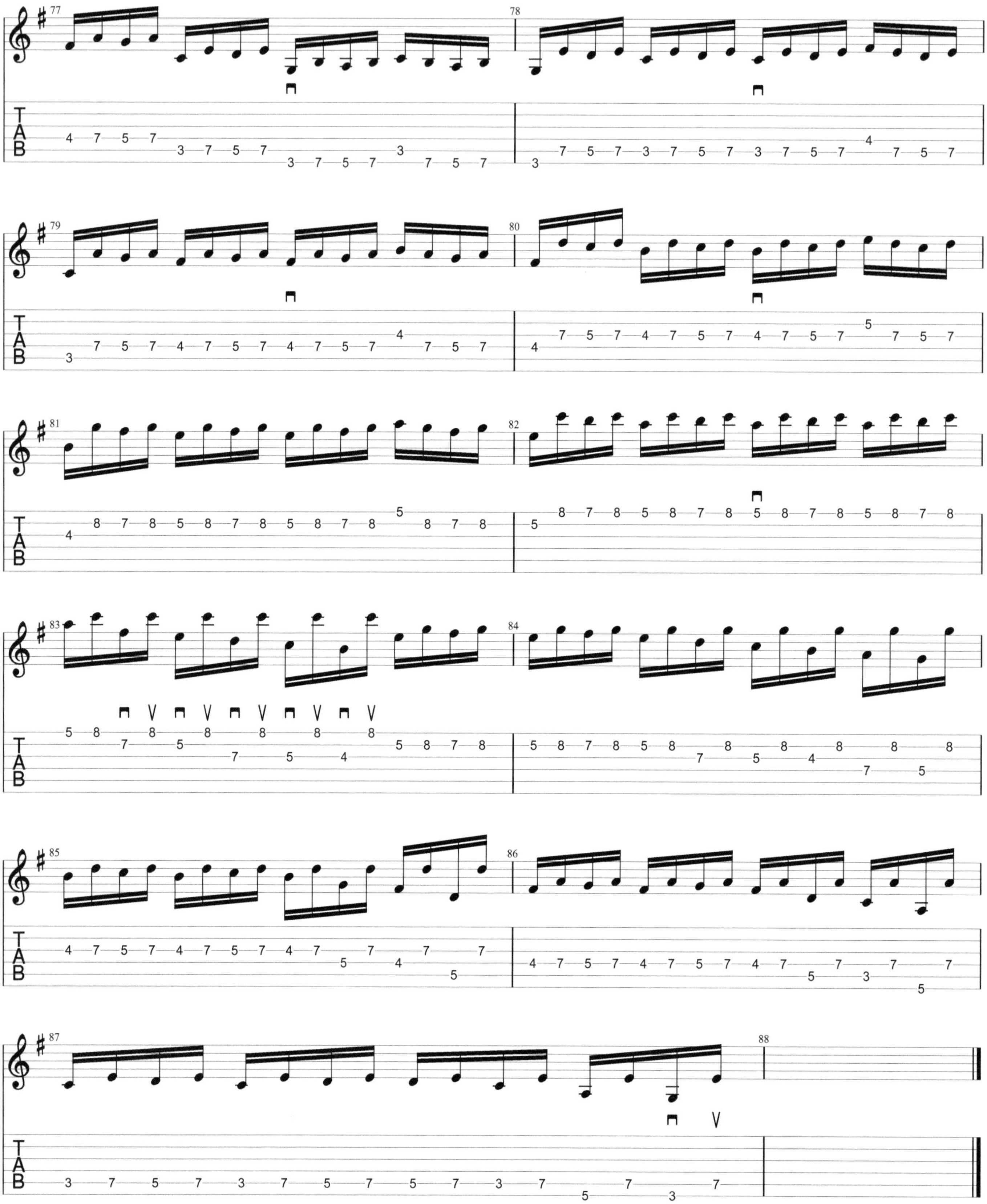

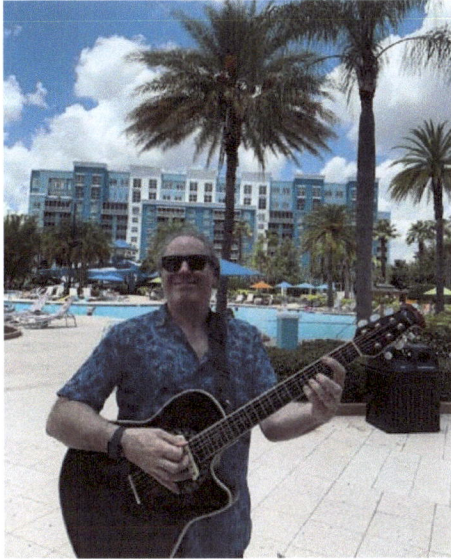

Author's Note

When I wrote my first book, I took some proven ideas and methods I had used with my own guitar students and organized them into a method book. Since the 1990s I was writing method books, yet, I never really knew what to do with them. I feel that I'm finally getting it right.

Computers and the internet have greatly changed everything for aspiring authors, guitarists and musicians across the world. I hope that I'm still learning and improving, both as a guitarist and a writer.

My first 3 books and website have changed my life. I feel luckier than ever to be able to play guitar live, and write for a living. I never take it for granted. That is why I must **thank you**, first and foremost.

Without you the reader, student, music fan, with your own quest for knowledge, this would not be possible.

Thank YOU!

Craig W. Smith
July 3rd, 2020

www.Lifein12Keys.com

Life in 12 Keys

Did you like this book? If so, please consider grabbing
one of my other books below.

Check out the Life In 12 Keys Guitar Book Store:
http://Books.Lifein12Keys.com

The 7 Day Practice Routine for Guitarists (2018) 92 Pages

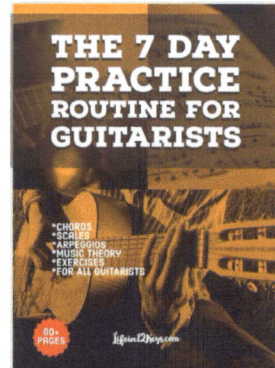

Guitar Chords for Beginners (2019) 36 Pages

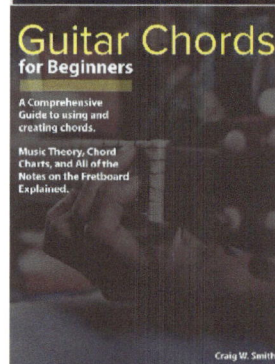

Classical Guitar - A Practical Guide Vol. 1 (2020) 129 Pages

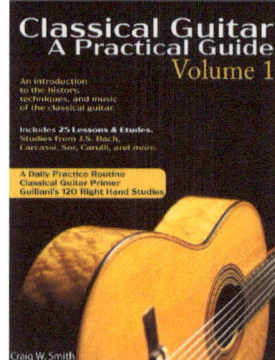

www.ingramcontent.com/pod-product-compliance
Lightning Source LLC
Chambersburg PA
CBHW061049090426
42740CB00002B/93